BEEN BANNED

ER PLANET

IN THE

GALAXY!

COKE OR PEPSI? UNIVERSE

DUDE

THE BOOK OF CRAZY, IMMATURE ST

WRITE! DRAW!

DESTROY!

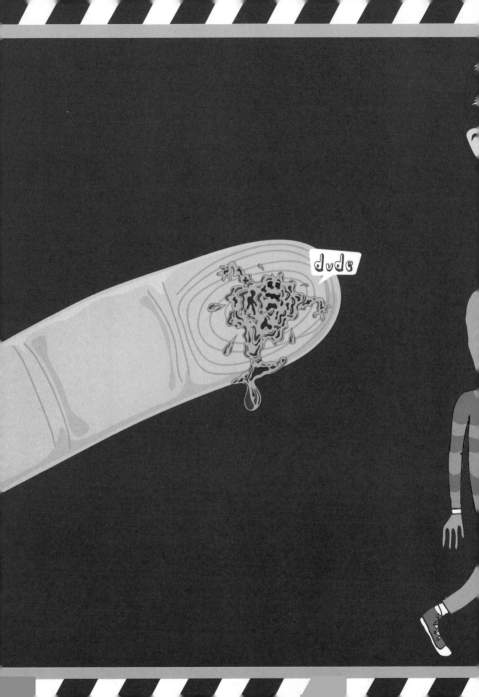

Written and designed by
Mickey & Cheryl Gill

Fine Print Publishing Company
P.O. Box 916401
Longwood, Florida 32791-6401

Created in the U.S.A. & Printed in China
This book is printed on acid-free paper.

ISBN 978-1-892951-46-5

Thanks to Brian (the Brain) Harris and his mom
Stephanie for bravely testing these pages.

10 9 8 7 6 5 4 3 2 1

thedudebook.com

VILLAINS!

Choose their crime

OIL SLICK

- ○ DUMPS OIL ON ROADS
- ○ DEEP-FRIES FOES
- ○ CAUSES PIMPLES ON TEENAGERS' FACES

TWISTED NINJA

- ○ SLICES & DICES
- ○ STIR-FRIES FOES
- ○ FLIPS OUT WHEN HE RUNS OUT OF SOY SAUCE

MASHER

- ○ POUNDS TO A PULP
- ○ MASHES FOES WITH POTATOES & BUTTER
- ○ GOES CRAZY WHEN THE GRAVY HAS LUMPS

○ HEAT VISION   ○ FREEZING BREATH   ○ INVULNERABILITY

SCARIEST SUPER VILLAIN?

WHAT WOULD BE THE ULTIMATE MATCH?

_____
SUPERHERO

VS.

_____
SUPER VILLAIN

HOW MANY DIFFERENT *SUPERHEROES* CAN YOU NAME?

_____   _____

_____   _____

_____   _____

_____   _____

_____   _____

_____   _____

_____   _____

_____   _____

_____   _____

○ SHRINK   ○ ENLARGE   ○ TELEKENESIS

_____   _____

_____   _____

_____   _____

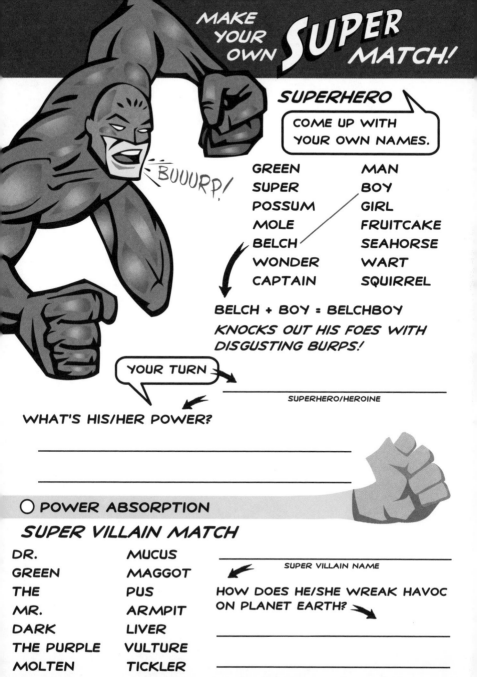

MAKE YOUR OWN SUPER MATCH!

BUUURP!

SUPERHERO

COME UP WITH YOUR OWN NAMES.

GREEN   MAN
SUPER   BOY
POSSUM   GIRL
MOLE   FRUITCAKE
BELCH   SEAHORSE
WONDER   WART
CAPTAIN   SQUIRREL

BELCH + BOY = BELCHBOY

KNOCKS OUT HIS FOES WITH DISGUSTING BURPS!

YOUR TURN

_____
SUPERHERO/HEROINE

WHAT'S HIS/HER POWER?

_____

_____

◯ POWER ABSORPTION

SUPER VILLAIN MATCH

DR.   MUCUS
GREEN   MAGGOT
THE   PUS
MR.   ARMPIT
DARK   LIVER
THE PURPLE   VULTURE
MOLTEN   TICKLER

_____
SUPER VILLAIN NAME

HOW DOES HE/SHE WREAK HAVOC ON PLANET EARTH?

_____

_____

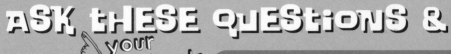

ASK tHESE QuESTiONS &

your friends

Ask your friends'
you might get in

Which is grosser?

1. ○ belly button lint
○ eye gunk

Which is grosser?

1 1/2. ○ gym socks
○ boogers

Which is grosser?

2. ○ grandma's mole
○ wet willy

You know ... when somebody sticks a finger in their mouth & then in your ear!

3. Ever eaten anything from the trash?

U know!
When there's a piece of cake or cookie just sitting on top ... YUM!

AHHH!
(someone's spit in your ear!)

By the way, spit
SMELLS!

● YES ● NO WAY

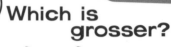

YOU'LL BE REALLY COOL!

MOMS these questions and trouble OR at least get a dirty look!

4. What's the longest you've ever gone without a bath?

_____

DUDE, YOU REEK!

Need a quick HALL PASS?
Impress your teacher with really big words!

_____
your teacher's name

May I be excused? I feel an odious bout of flatulence coming upon me.

FORGOT TO DO YOUR HOMEWORK?

I WAS WORKING ON MY HOMEWORK IN MY BACKYARD WHEN SUDDENLY A BIRD SNATCHED IT OUT OF MY HAND AND LINED HER NEST WITH IT. AWESOME, HUH?

THE CLASSIC CANINE EXCUSE

HOMEWORK HAS REALLY BEEN EATING INTO MY QUALITY FAMILY TIME. SO LAST NIGHT I DECIDED TO PUT MY LOVED ONES FIRST.

I JUST COULDN'T PUT DOWN MY REQUIRED READING BOOK. IT'S SO CAPTIVATING. I'M THINKING OF STARTING A BOOK CLUB. SO, I KINDA FORGOT TO DO MY HOMEWORK.

USING THE WORD "IMPLODE" IS ALWAYS BETTER THAN "EXPLODE" WHEN TALKING TO TEACHERS. THEY'LL THINK YOU'VE BEEN STUDYING SOMETHING.

I WAS SUFFERING FROM MENTAL FATIGUE LAST NIGHT. IT FELT LIKE MY BRAIN WOULD IMPLODE IF ANY MORE INFORMATION WENT INTO IT.

CAPTIVATE - A COOL VERB. IT MEANS TO ATTRACT & HOLD THE ATTENTION OF. YOU SEE IT IN A LOT OF THOSE KISSING BOOKS GIRLS LIKE. WHATEVER.

CONFISCATE - ANOTHER VERB. IT MEANS TO TAKE SOMEONE'S PROPERTY, WITH AUTHORITY. GUARDS DO IT ALL THE TIME. AT LEAST ON TV, THEY DO.

THE PAPER I WROTE WAS SUCH A STROKE OF GENIUS THAT IT WAS CONFISCATED BY THE CIA, FBI, OR SOME GROUP OF IMPORTANT SPY-LIKE GUYS.

If you Were

WHAT WOULD YOU WANT TO DO?

1. ____________________

2. ____________________

3. ____________________

4. ____________________

5. ____________________

- **Stand next to your family pet & rat out your sister or brother**
- Stand next to your family pet during breakfast & scream "THIS FOOD ISN'T FIT FOR A ROACH! I'll have what you're having."
- STAND BEHIND SOMEONE CHECKING THEMSELF OUT IN A MIRROR AND SAY, "WOW! YOU LOOK AWFUL!"

Do you believe in ghosts?

- Nah, it's all made up
- Yeah
- Yep, seen one

a ghost,

☞ SPY ON PEOPLE

☞ sneak up behind your parents and yell "BOO!"

Who else would you like to hose down?

_____
_____
_____

These only work with those invisible kind of ghosts ... not those white cloudy kind you see on TV— whatever!

☞ SQUIRT KIDS THAT WALK IN FRONT OF YOUR HOUSE WITH A HOSE

☞ Go up to a bully @ school & give him a wedgie!

☞ Hang out in the TEACHERS' LOUNGE and whisper things like "Do not assign homework."

How 'bout haunted houses?
● Nah
● Well, i said yes to ghosts.

The Coolest

VIDEO GAME _____

THING YOU CAN DO WITH A MEATBALL

_____

(that's not a cartoon)
TV SHOW _____

OK, NOW A CARTOON _____

MOVIE _____

SINGER OR BAND _____

WAY TO GET OUT OF TROUBLE _____

_____

(that uses a ball)
SPORT _____

(that doesn't
use a ball)
SPORT _____

SUPERSTAR ATHLETE _____

The Worst

CAFETERIA FOOD _____

If you're eating it right now, wipe a little here

SINGER/BAND _____

SCHOOL SUBJECT _____

THING ABOUT GIRLS _____

THING YOU EVER DID & GOT IN TROUBLE FOR _____

_____

VIDEO GAME EVER _____

(that of course you never watch!)
TV SHOW _____

MOVIE EVER _____

(that uses a ball)
SPORT _____

(that doesn't use a ball)
SPORT _____

DRIVEN MAD BY MONSTERS!

ULTIMATE CREEPY MONSTER?

☐ FRANKENSTEIN ☐ DRACULA

☐ MUMMY ☐ WEREWOLF

☐ OTHER _____

WHY IS IT THE CREEPIEST? _____

If you were a werewolf, would you tell anyone?

☐ no way! ☐ yes. Who? _____

WORST THING ABOUT BEING A VAMPIRE?

☐ sleeping during the day in very tight quarters, a.k.a. a coffin

☐ that big black cape

☐ drinking blood! yuck!

☐ really bad overbite

☐ highly allergic to garlic

☐ always running from people with steaks

(I think it's S-T-A-K-E-S)

WHAT FREAKS YOU OUT MOST ABOUT WITCHES?

☐ Magical powers ☐ Nasty hair

☐ Cauldron of eyeballs, bones, pieces, & of course, eye of newt

☐ WARTS! AHHHH!!

THE BEST

SODA _____ →

Dribble some here

Smear some here →

CANDY BAR _____

FAST FOOD PLACE _____

TEAM FOR –

    FOOTBALL _____

    BASEBALL _____

    BASKETBALL _____

    HOCKEY _____

    SOCCER _____

    BOBSLEDDING _____

ICE CREAM FLAVOR _____

PIZZA TOPPING _____

THING ABOUT GIRLS _____

RIDE YOU'VE EVER BEEN ON _____

GROSS THING TO DO WHEN NO ONE'S PAYING ATTENTION

    ○ Pick your nose   ○ Let one rip

    ○ Belch   ○ Bite your toenails

The Lamest

STORE AT THE MALL _____

CEREAL INVENTED _____

FAST FOOD PLACE _____

TEAM FOR —

    FOOTBALL _____

    BASEBALL _____

    BASKETBALL _____

    HOCKEY _____

    SOCCER _____

    WATER POLO _____ (Are there horses involved?)

FIELD TRIP EVER _____

RIDE YOU'VE EVER BEEN ON _____

BOOK YOU'VE EVER READ _____

VACATION YOU'VE EVER TAKEN _____

THING A PARENT MAKES YOU EAT _____

_____

MASTERS OF

**Concentrate really hard ...
can you list all of the
video games
you've ever played?**

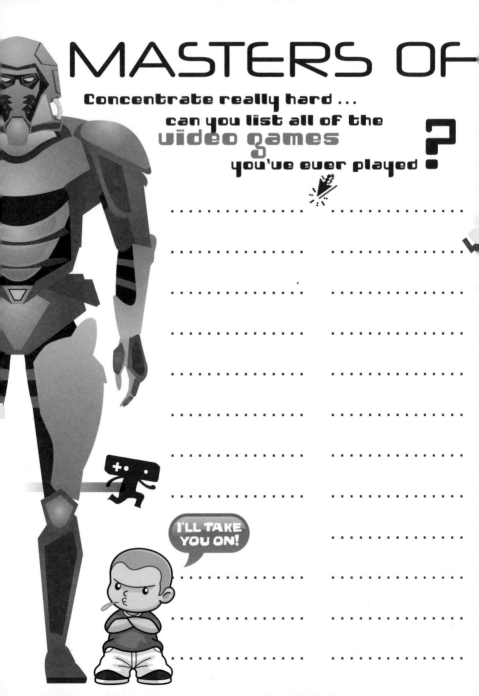

I'LL TAKE
YOU ON!

THE GAME

Coolest Gaming character?

WHAT ARE YOUR TOP 3 FAVORITES?

Coolest Racing game

1
2
3

Coolest Sports game

Which game R U best at?

Game with the sweetest prizes?

Into CHEAT CODES?
○ NAH ○ YEAH - 4 WHICH GAMES?

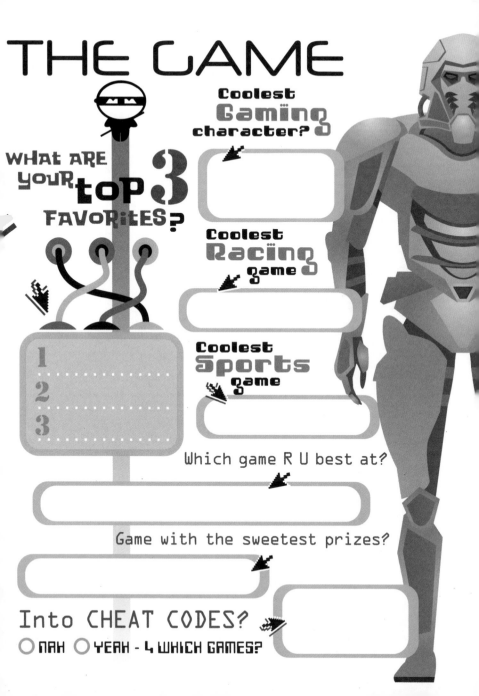

GAMING

Ever hurt your hand gaming too much?

○ nah
○ oh yeah

Longest you've ever gamed (in hours dude, not days)?

[   ]

Ever play against some-one in another state?

○ no
○ yeah, where?

[   ]

UNLIMITED

When gaming, who do you like to team up with?

Who do you like to face off against most?

Another country?
O no
O yeah (where?)

THE ULTIM

Out of all your friends
who deserves the
Most Awesome Gamer Title?

_____

WHICH GROWN-UPS
SOUND FAMILIAR?
[CHECK ALL THAT APPLY]

Put that control down & go get some fresh air!

COOL, let's play some Rock Band!

Whatever happened to tossing a football around?

I think gaming helps develop motor skills.

BEST PLACE TO
GAME IN THE NEIGHBORHOOD?

_____

ATE GAME

dude

WHICH GAMES ARE THE SWEETEST?

- ○ **ACTION!**
- ○ **SCI-FI**
- ○ **FANTASY**
- ○ **PUZZLES**
- ○ **MUSIC**

- ○ **ROCK BAND®**

  OR

- ○ **GUITAR HERO®**

IF YOU COULD DESIGN A VIDEO GAME WHAT WOULD IT BE ABOUT?

WHAT WOULD YOU CALL IT?

CHORE-AVOIDING CHECKLIST

Here are some crazy attempts to get out of chores.
(Don't get any ideas dude. They won't work.)

☐ **Rake Leaves** "Don't chiggers live in piles of dead leaves? What if they get on me? Don't they hide in all the warm parts of your body? I've heard they like underwear."

☐ **Clean Bedroom** "I think I'm allergic to dust mites. I notice a lot of postnasal drip every time I clean my room. I think it's best if I don't disturb the mites."

☐ **Walk the Dog** "I'm really not the best pooper scooper. Something might get on my hands, like it did last time. And you know, you're always bugging me and saying I don't wash my hands enough. "

☐ **Take Out the Garbage** "Aren't flies attracted to garbage? If they lay eggs, won't they become maggots? I don't know exactly what maggots do, but people's faces always scrunch up when you say 'maggots.'"

☐ **Fold Clothes** "I'm not really good at folding. If my clothes were folded correctly by someone who was really good at it, think of all the ironing that could be avoided."

If you were in **CHARGE,**
what chores would you enforce ?
Who would do them? Would they be paid?

I would make my little sister smell each of my dirty, stinky gym socks before she sorted them into nice, neat piles. Ha!

Duck + Bat = Quackbat

_____ + _____ = _____
Animal   Animal   New Creature

_____ + _____ = _____   **MAD!**
Animal   Animal   New Creature

_____ + _____ = _____
Animal   Animal   New Creature

_____ + _____ = _____
Animal   Animal   New Creature

ARE YOU CRAZY!

_____ + _____ = _____
Animal   Animal   New Creature

Science

I'm skeledog.
I eat bullies!

Technically,
a skeleton is not
a monster, but
hey, it's cool.

Now,
cross a Monster
with an animal!

Likes
to eat

			EATS	
Monster	+ Animal	= New Creature		Food

			EATS	
Monster	+ Animal	= New Creature		Food

YUCK!

			EATS	
Monster	+ Animal	= New Creature		Food

			EATS	
Monster	+ Animal	= New Creature		Food

			EATS	
Monster	+ Animal	= New Creature		Food

IF YOU COULD
FEED A

burp

V·nus fly·trap
noun

a **carnivorous** bog plant with hinged leaves that spring shut on and **digest** insects that land on them. Native to the Southern U.S., it is also kept as an indoor plant.

GIANT VENUS FLYTRAP

that ATE absolutely anything - what would you give it

My Flytrap food list

Not your little sister, creep!

_____ eeew! _____

_____   _____

_____   _____

_____   _____

_____   _____

CASTAWAY ON A DESERT ISLAND

YOU'RE STUCK ON A DESERT ISLAND IN THE MIDDLE OF A HUGE OCEAN FULL OF SHARKS! ONE GOOD THING, SOMEONE LEFT A DESALINATOR BEHIND. THAT'S A COOL SCIENCE PROJECT THAT CHANGES SALT WATER INTO DRINKING WATER. SWEET! LEARN HOW TO FISH & YOU JUST MIGHT SURVIVE.

YOU CAN HAVE A FEW THINGS FROM HOME.

What beverage would you like to drink on the island? (besides your fresh water)

1 food item?
(besides all the fish you can catch)

You can listen to all the songs of 1 singer or band. Who do you pick?

Game? (Yes, you'll have a system to play it on!)

Book or comic book series?

HOW WOULD YOU TRY TO GET BACK HOME?

- Build a bonfire (Be careful, you could burn the whole island down!)
- Spell out H-E-L-P with sticks in the sand (Watch the tides!)
- Try to build a boat & sail to freedom (Can you build anything?)
- Other

HELP!

A monkey becomes your pet. What would u call 'im?
- ○ BOB
- ○ MONKEY FACE
- ○ MR. GIGGLES
- ○ OTHER _____

What would you train your monkey sidekick to do?
- ○ Fish
- ○ Sign language (Wait, do you know it?)
- ○ Pat his head & rub his stomach at the same time! *What? I need to have SOME fun!*
- ○ Fetch me bananas & coconuts
- ○ Other _____

COOLEST THING ABOUT ISLAND LIVING?
- ○ THE BEACH, 24/7
- ○ NO BEDROOM TO CLEAN
- ○ NO GARBAGE TO TAKE OUT
- ○ NO SCHOOL
- ○ MY PET MONKEY CAN WALK HIMSELF & POOP WHEREVER HE WANTS
- ○ OTHER _____

WORST THING ABOUT ISLAND LIVING?
- ○ OUCH! THE SUNBURN
- ● FIXING MY OWN MEALS
- ● SPEAKING OF MEALS ... FISH, FISH & MORE FISH, UGH!
- ● A MONKEY NAMED
  _____
  IS MY ONLY FRIEND
- ● ALWAYS HAVING SAND IN MY UNDERWEAR

WOULD U
- ○ EAT SUSHI
- ○ LEARN HOW TO START A FIRE & MAKE GRILLED MAHI-MAHI?

IF YOU WERE A GROWN-UP, WHAT WOULD YOU FORBID?

1. Do Not _____

2. Do Not _____

3. Do Not _____

4. Do Not _____

5. Do Not _____

Do not yell at kids under 16.

WOULD YOU RATHER ...

BE STUCK FOR HOURS IN A CAR FULL OF

☐ GUYS WHO ATE A BUNCH OF BEAN BURRITOS

☐ GIRLS ALL WEARING DIFFERENT **OR** PERFUMES AND TALKING NON-STOP?

HAVE A
BAD CASE OF
☐ **POISON IVY** **OR**
☐ **ATHLETE'S FOOT?**

You could **NOT** talk. You could avoid lifting your arms up.

Have really
☐ **bad breath**
OR
☐ **stinky armpits?**

Spend the night in a room that smelled like
☐ cat pee **OR** ☐ dog poo?

LEASE! e right thing | PET POOP | ANIMAL Toilet Here | DOG WASTE | CLEAN UP After your Dog

What kind of

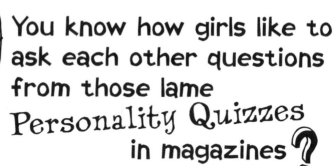

You know how girls like to ask each other questions from those lame Personality Quizzes in magazines?

Well, here's one . . . and it's way easier & more AWESOME.

This is what you do.

1. Look at the 2 choices on the next page.

2. Decide who you are more like. Put a check in the circle next to it.

3. Turn the book upside down to reveal your personality.

dude are you?

○ SpongeBob SquarePants

○ Patrick Star

What kind of BEST

who? me?

OK, now that you know what kind of dude YOU are, figure out your best friend. (Girls call them BFFs.)

Dude, that's dumb.

1. See the 2 choices on the next page?

2. Pick the one that's most like your friend.

3. If you can read this, then you've turned the book upside down. Can you see the answers on the other page?

dude is your FRIEND?

(Think sidekick)

I NEED AARDVARK MAN

anything you can't stand! →

to come suck up

& SAVE ME FROM PERIL!

If 👁 had a **ROBOT,** I would

program it to
- [ ] do all my homework
- [ ] dispense my favorite candy 24/7
- [ ] carry my backpack
- [ ] stand up to jerks
- [ ] only make pizza for dinner
- [ ] other_____

YOU HAVE 3 WISHES.

I wish that...

1. _____ came out of my mouth when i **burped!**

2. my **farts** _____ when i let one.

3. Boogers turned into

_____

when you picked one.

SPEAKING OF STUPID...

SPEAKING OF DUMB...

Just How Many Different Names Do You Know For This Bodily Function?

(when you run out of names, ask around and find out some more.)

_____   _____

_____   _____

_____   _____

_____   _____

_____   _____

_____   _____

The gas you pass

You swallow air when you eat & drink & even chew gum. It goes into your intestines and makes gas.

Everything doesn't always get digested in your small intestine. So, it goes down to your large intestine. Bacteria break it down and make gas.

Whether it's air or broken down stuff, YOU'RE FULL O' GAS.

Gas is propelled down through your intestines and then it's forced out. BRAP!

When you let one fly, it's a cool combo of oxygen, nitrogen, hydrogen, carbon dioxide and methane. (Dude, that sounds like a bomb!)

10-20 air bombs a day is NORMAL!

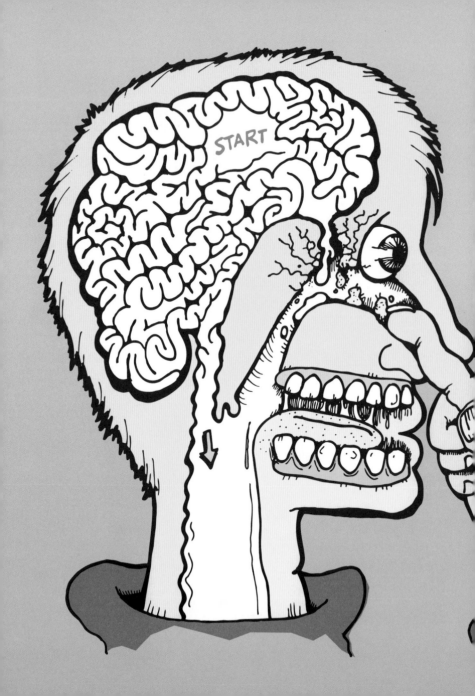

OK, NOW HOW MANY NAMES DO YOU KNOW FOR THE YELLOW STUFF THAT COMES OUT OF YOUR NOSE AND sometimes even your mouth?

_____   _____

_____   _____

_____   _____

_____   _____

Have you ever . . .

been caught picking your nose? ⬤ no way ⬤ of course!

been hit by a loogie from someone's sneeze?

⬤ yes, gross! ⬤ nope

had GREEN stuff in your nose?

⬤ yep (DUDE! were you really sick?) ⬤ nah

measured the distance you can hock a loogie?

⬤ yep. How far can you? _____ ⬤ no

at last, THE MOTHER

They ask,

"Will you come with US?"

You reply,

- ○ "Not right now. Thursday night is chicken fingers. Try me later dude."

- ○ "No way man!" (Then run 4 your life!)

- ○ "Cool. Let me get my phone."

- ○ "Sure, can I bring a friend? How 'bout my dog?"

What would you like to ask the little guys?
↓

_____

_____

_____

SHiP HaS aRRiVeD

Do you believe there is life on other planets?

○ Um, yeah, right!
○ Yes!

Think you've seen a UFO?

○ Nope
○ Absolutely

What did you see? →

Whadaya think aliens look like?
↓

_____

_____

_____

Better yet, turn the page and draw some. →

Draw what you think aliens look like

(or would look like if you thought they were Real.)

SWEET

If you could buy a car or motorcycle, right here, right now, AND you had the money for it (even a really expensive one), what would you get?

STO

Can't decide on just 1?
That's cool. Make a list of
cars/motorcycles/planes/spacecraft/etc.
you'd like to own:

RIDE

Best car color?

Friends' favorite cars & motorcycles?

Sweetest car feature?

○ convertible top   ○ heated seats! *oh yeah!*
○ satellite radio   ○ 0-60 in 8 seconds
○ other_____

I want a car that

○ can shoot laser beams
   from the headlights

○ is voice-
   activated

○ can convert
   into a boat
   with the flip
   of a switch

○ other_____

_____

_____

_____

ONE WAY ➤

Lamest car?

Movie/TV character with the coolest car/motorcycle?

Racing Fan? ○ Nah ○ Yeah!
What kind?

Ever been to a race?
○ Nope ○ Yep *It was sweet!*

What's the most awesome thing about the Batmobile?

○ front autocannons
○ rocket launcher
○ jet engine on back for quick boosts
○ stealth mode
○ Batpod cycle ejects from front wheels
○ other_____

Ask yourself & your friends this question.

Write down the answers.

_____

_____

_____

_____

_____

_____

_____

_____

_____

_____

Turn the page

Ask everyone who answered your
"worst pain ever" survey
to vote on the best story.

We crown

Dude's name

THE KING of PAIN.
AAAAAAHHH!

Pain in my Butt!

(Check all of the pains you've ever felt.)

- O bee sting
- O wasp sting
- O jellyfish sting
- O ant bite
- O mosquito bite
- O spider bite
- O snake bite
- O dog bite
- O cat bite
- O shark bite
- O little kid bite
- O cat scratch
- O sunburn
- O busted lip
- O black eye
- O broken arm
- O broken nose

- O broken leg
- O broken finger
- O broken toe
- O nail in the foot
- O ball on the head
- O iron burn
- O stove burn
- O paper cut
- O gaping wound
- O stitches for gaping wound
- O spanking! yow!
- O pulled muscle
- O splinter
- O pink eye!
- O ear ache
- O toothache

the GROSSEST

Thing that ever happened 2 me!

"I had to go on a road trip with my family. Grandma kept ripping air bombs in the car... for 5 hours!

"My little sister ate a bowl of corn flakes and went on a merry-go-round. Then she barfed ALL over me! It reeked!"

"I CUT MY LEG OPEN & had to get stitches. It got all infected and full of yellow pus."

Ask all of your friends what's the grossest thing that's ever happened to them.
Include yourself.

Write down each story here.

Turn the page

Now, ask your buds to choose
who deserves the noble & nasty
title of the

KING of DISGUST!

Dude's name

Which is more disgusting?

1. ○ ROAD KILL **or** ○ VULTURES

2. BABY ○ DIAPERS (fully loaded)
   or
   ○ SPIT-UP

3. ○ GRANDMA'S PERFUME **or**
   ○ GRANDPA'S NOSE HAIR

4. KITTY ○ HAIRBALLS
   or
   ○ LITTER BOX

5. ○ NOSE **or** ○ SCAB PICKER

Let's Eat!

You get to hang out & eat dinner with ANY people (& creatures) in the world! who would you choose?

5

#1 One of your friends

_____
name

#2 Famous athlete

_____
name

#3 Make-believe creature

_____
name

#4 Book or movie character

_____
name

#5 Movie star or famous singer/band member

_____
name

Where would you eat?

_____

What would you eat?

_____

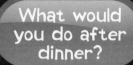

What would you do after dinner?

- get everyone's autographs
- play video games
- watch a movie
- get out of the make-believe creature's way

Write a list of questions you would ask your guests (not including your friend of course).

_____

_____

_____

_____

_____

_____

What's a T-shirt?

My Threads

Have a favorite T-shirt? ⚪no ⚪yes

What is it? ⬡ ▭

Do you ever put dirty clothes BACK on?
⚪ oh yeah ⚪ nah, they reek!

Have a favorite pair of shorts or pants? ⚪no ⚪yes

If you answered YES to question above,
what are they? ⬡ ▭

Wear them so much that your family hates them?
⚪ yep ⚪ nope

Where do your sneakers register on a smell-o-meter? ○ unsmelly ○ pretty stinky ○ off-the-charts disgusting!

Wear socks with holes in them? ○ yeah, who cares? ○ nah

Wear shirts with holes in them? ○ yes ○ no, not allowed to ○ no, I'm not that bad

Ever had to wear a tie or bow tie? ○ no ○ yes
Did it just about strangle you? ○ yes ○ no

What's something you would NEVER wear?

Buurp!

How Gross R

let a big one rip on purpose? ○ nah ○ of course!

Belch to annoy someone in your family? ○ yep ○ no

Pick your nose in public?

○ yes, who cares?! ○ no

Ever "gone" on the side of the road?

○ sure ○ no

Bite your toenails? ○ yes

○ no, how do you even do that?

You?

Stick chewed gum under desks? ○ yes ○ no

Wipe your hands on your shirt? ○ all the time ○ no

E

Pick scabs? ○ yes, but I'm not proud of it ○ no

S

Ever "gone" in the pool? ○ sure ○ no

Eat stuff you drop on the floor? ○ yep ○ nope

Tasted dog or cat food? ○ yes ○ no

I can't reach my head.

How Talented R

Can you whistle a tune?
○ no ○ yes! (let's hear it.)

Can you stand on your hands?
○ yes ○ no

Know how to fish? ○ no ○ yes
Caught anything? ○ no ○ yes. (What?)

[ ]

?sdrawkcab daer uoy naC ○ yes ○ no

Tell any good jokes? ○ nope
○ yes! (Let's hear 1.)

[ ]

You?

Know how to play cards?
○ not really ○ yes

What can you play?

Rub your stomach & pat your head at the same time? ○ yes ○ no

Won a thumb wrestling match? ○ yes ○ no

Write your first name backwards with the hand that's NOT your writing hand?
○ no ○ yes! (let's see it!)

coke or pepsi? universe

I'm the Hulk!

The Cooler Dude

Who would you choose?

- You   ○ Your Best Friend
- Ninja   ○ Pirate
- Mermaid Man   ○ Barnacle Boy
- Iron Man   ○ Superman
- Harry Potter   ○ Gandalf
- Wolverine   ○ The Hulk
- SpongeBob   ○ Patrick
- Batman   ○ Spider-Man
- Obi-Wan   ○ Mace Windu
- You   ○ The Coolest Kid In School

Stuff Your Face

Whadaya like best?

- ○ Cake ○ Icing
- ○ Chocolate-Chip Cookies ○ Brownies
- ○ Coke ○ Pepsi
- ○ Hot Dog ○ Hamburger
- ○ Taco ○ Burrito
- ○ Creamy ○ Crunchy Peanut Butter
- ○ Big Mac ○ Whopper
- ○ Pizza ○ Spaghetti
- ○ Plain ○ Peanut M&M'S
- ○ Cinnamon Roll ○ Donut
- ○ Chocolate ○ Vanilla

GOOD DUDES

which star wars movies have you seen?
rank them in order of awesomeness!
(#1 is the best and #7 is your least favorite.)

- [ ] episode 1: the phantom menace
- [ ] episode 2: attack of the clones
- [ ] episode 3: revenge of the sith
- [ ] episode 4: a new hope
- [ ] episode 5: the empire strikes back
- [ ] episode 6: return of the jedi
- [ ] star wars: the clone wars

who's the funniest? (it could be how they talk, look, whatever.)

- [ ] chewbacca (& wookiees in general)
- [ ] jar jar binks
- [ ] ewoks
- [ ] jabba the hutt
- [ ] other_____

if you could ask yoda 1 question about absolutely anything, what would you ask him?

```
[                                    ]
```

BAD DUDES
IN A GALAXY FAR, FAR AWAY

Ask some random adults if they know what the name of the weapon is that Luke Skywalker uses.

Write down how many of them gave these answers:

☐ **Lightsaber** (Congratulate them for the correct answer.)

☐ **Life Saver** (Tell them life savers are candy and would be a stupid thing to go into battle with.)

☐ **Life Saber** (Just snicker and walk away.)

COOL DUDES

think about all the star wars movies
and their characters ...

how many good guys/girls/creatures can you name?

_____

_____

_____

_____

_____

_____

_____

_____

_____

who's your favorite?

EVILDOER DUDES

how many bad guys/girls/creatures can you name?

_____

_____

_____

_____

_____

_____

_____

_____

_____

who's your favorite?

MISSION:

you're a **JEDI** getting ready for a mission. you need to choose a weapon (for defense only), someone to join you, a droid and a starship. (by the way, you can cross space and time — you can choose a partner and a starship from different movies.)

TAKE ON

write in foe

and KICK SOME BUTT!

who will you defend the GALAXY FROM?

darth sidious (chancellor palpatine who becomes the emperor)

darth tyranus (count dooku)

darth maul

asajj ventress

general grievous

darth vader (anakin skywalker)

jabba the hutt

the epic continues

Plan your

you get to choose 1 weapon to defend yourself. (ok, so some of these are from the dark side, but you will only use them for good & to defend yourself. remember, you're a jedi dude!) which 1 would you choose?

- [ ] lightsaber
- [ ] paired lightsabers
- [ ] electrostaff
- [ ] blaster pistol
- [ ] blaster rifle
- [ ] arc welder
- [ ] buzz saw
- [ ] dark side lightning

choose someone to join you on the mission...

- [ ] qui-gon jinn
- [ ] mace windu
- [ ] (obi-wan) ben kenobi
- [ ] anakin skywalker (pre-darth vader days, dude!)
- [ ] padmé amidala
- [ ] luke skywalker
- [ ] princess leia organa
- [ ] han solo
- [ ] lando calrissian
- [ ] chewbacca
- [ ] other

MISSION

now choose 1 droid ...

■ C-3PO (cool protocol droid)

OR

■ R2-D2 (packed with gadgets and
always entertaining)

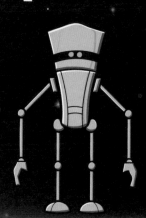

and finally, choose your starship ...

■ jedi starfighter (episodes 2 & 3 & clone wars)

■ twilight (anakin's souped-up space transport in clone wars)

■ x-wing starfighter (episodes 4, 5 & 6)

■ millennium falcon (episodes 4, 5 & 6)

■ a-wing starfighter (episode 6)

■ b-wing starfighter (episode 6)

■ other

How to make a sugar-coated work of art.

1. Eat one of those really shocking, bright-colored candies.

2. Check out your tongue in a mirror. Make sure it's a really bright color.

3. Press your tongue on a clean piece of white paper (you know, the non-toxic kind). Now you have a tongue stamp.

4. Cut out your stamp.

5. Tape to this page.

Tape the book open on a table or something outside.
Or put 2 rocks on it so it stays open.

Back up pretty far and try to spit on the book. (Like when you hock a loogie, but don't actually hock a loogie!).

Keep moving forward until you actually hit the book with some sweet saliva.

Measure the distance and write it on the page.

If spit just falls on your shoe, you're a lame spitter.
Try spitting a watermelon seed instead.

My Foul Footwriting

Hold a thin marker between your toes.
(Between whatever toes feel comfortable, dude!)

Try to write something like — FOOT ODOR — on this page.
(Someone may have to hold the book open for you. So,
make sure your feet really stink.)

Now, try to remove the marker from between your toes, using only your teeth. (If you can't or are too wimpy and think it's gross, just use your hands!)

Using your teeth, try to write something like — TOE BREATH — on this page. You'll probably drool all over the page.

Check your sneakers for dirt or dust.
The dirtier, the better. Place book on the floor & step on this page.
Cool.

I Live with

Go around your house & collect stuff.
Wipe your finger across your drawers, collect dust bunnies,
dead bugs & whatever.
Tape them here.

My C██████████ heels

Run over this page with whatever you're riding.

○ Bike   ○ Skateboard   ○ Scooter   ○ Dirt bike

○ Other _____

You'll probably have to duct tape the book down first.
Or, ask two of your very best friends to hold the pages
open for you. Yeah, right.

Here's your chance to leave your dirty fingerprints all over something and NOT get into trouble.

1. Get your hands really dirty.

2. Press your thumbs down on this page. Make sure you leave some prints.

3. Whatever you do, DO NOT draw little stick arms and legs on your thumbprints. Cuz that's just dumb.

What's your favorite deep-fried potato?

○ **Chips**

○ Fries

1. Place a chip or fry here.
2. Close the book.
3. Smash it.
4. Dump food out.
5. Admire your grease work!
(Hey! It won't work with those healthy "baked" chips.)

Write something here that you don't tell everyone, but wouldn't be a big deal if the whole world knew. Huh?

Kinda seal your "not-so-secret" secret with gum on the next page.

BONUS! Hidden Gum Compartment

Stick a wad of gum down each time it loses its flavor.
Soon, you'll have a pocket to store really important stuff in.

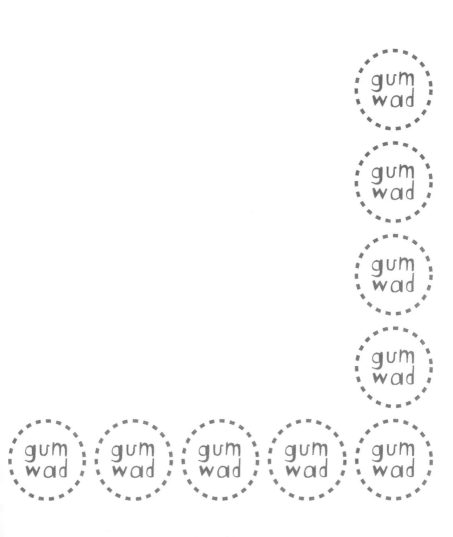

JIBBER JABBER

WHAT WORD DO YOU & YOUR FRIENDS SAY THE MOST?

(If you can't think of 1, ask your family or your friends.)

The envelope please,
the overused word of the century is...

DUDE.

POKE HOLES IN THIS PAGE RIGHT HERE

tear out this page. Ball it up. Bean your friend, brother, sister, cat or dog on the head with it.

STICK THIS STUFF UP IN YOUR LOCKER, BEDROOM &, OH YEAH, BATHROOM

Go to
THEDUDEBOOK.COM
to download more copies.

⚠ CAUTION

Hazardous Gas

Avoid vapors and direct contact. Wear protective equipment.

Cut out and tape to your bathroom door when the air's not too fresh inside.

CAUTION

BLASTING AREA
KEEP AWAY

Cut out and tape to the bathroom door.

WARNING

PROPERTY CONTAINS FILTH.

POISONOUS FUMES MAY FORM WHEN COMBINED WITH CLEANING SOLUTIONS.

Cut out and tape to your bedroom door.

Cut out and tape to your bedroom door.

Cut out and tape to area where a possible Bigfoot crossing may occur.

Cut out and tape to area where a possible alien crossing may occur.

SECURITY NOTICE

IF YOU ARE DUMPING ILLEGALLY SMILE FOR THE CAMERA

Cut out and tape to the INSIDE of your bathroom door.

UNAUTHORIZED DUMPING OF ANY MATERIAL IS PROHIBITED

Cut out and tape to the OUTSIDE of your bathroom door.

Cut out and tape to your bedroom door.

NO TRESPASSING

GUARD TRICERATOPS ON DUTY

Cut out and tape to wherever you want.

Cut out and tape to the trash can.

FRESH

HANDPICKED
BOOGERS
INSIDE

Cut out and tape to anything you don't want people to touch.

Cut out and tape to anywhere you do not want an alien invasion to occur.

NO
FARTING

Cut out and tape to whatever you want.